AQUARIUS

AQUARIUS

21 January–19 February

PATTY GREENALL & CAT JAVOR

MQP

Published by MQ Publications Limited
12 The Ivories
6–8 Northampton Street
London N1 2HY
Tel: 020 7359 2244
Fax: 020 7359 1616
Email: mail@mqpublications.com
Website: www.mqpublications.com

Copyright © MQ Publications Limited 2004
Text copyright © Patty Greenall & Cat Javor 2004

Illustrations: Gerry Baptist

ISBN: 1-84072-659-8

1 3 5 7 9 0 8 6 4 2

Printed in Italy

1 THE **ESSENTIAL** AQUARIUS

2 **RISING** SIGNS

3 **RELATION**SHIPS

WHAT IS **ASTROLOGY**?

Astrology is the practice of interpreting the positions and movements of celestial bodies with regard to what they can tell us about life on Earth. In particular it is the study of the cycles of the Sun, Moon, and the planets of our solar system, and their journeys through the twelve signs of the zodiac—Aries, Taurus, Gemini, Cancer, Leo, Virgo, Libra, Scorpio, Sagittarius, Capricorn, Aquarius, and Pisces—all of which provide astrologers with a rich diversity of symbolic information and meaning.

Astrology has been labeled a science, an occult magical practice, a religion, and an art, yet it cannot be confined by any one of these descriptions. Perhaps the best way to describe it is as an evolving tradition.

Throughout the world, for as far back as history can inform us, people have been looking up at the skies and attaching stories and meanings to what they see there. Neolithic peoples in Europe built huge stone structures such as Stonehenge in southern England in order to plot the cycles of the Sun and Moon, cycles that were so important to a fledgling agricultural society. There are star-lore traditions in the ancient cultures of India, China, South America, and Africa, and among the indigenous people of Australia. The ancient Egyptians plotted the rising of the star Sirius, which marked the annual flooding of the Nile, and in ancient Babylon, astronomer-priests would perform astral divination in the service of their king and country.

Since its early beginnings, astrology has grown, changed, and diversified into a huge body of knowledge that has been added to by many learned men and women throughout history. It has continued to evolve and become richer and more informative, despite periods when it went out of favor because of religious, scientific, and political beliefs.

Offering us a deeper knowledge of ourselves, a profound insight into what motivates, inspires, and, in some cases, hinders, our ability to be truly our authentic selves, astrology equips us better to make the choices and decisions that confront us daily. It is a wonderful tool, which can be applied to daily life and our understanding of the world around us.

The horoscope—or birth chart—is the primary tool of the astrologer and the position of the Sun, Moon, Mercury, Venus, Mars, Jupiter, Saturn,

Uranus, Neptune, and Pluto at the moment a person was born are all considered when one is drawn up. Each planet has its own domain, affinities, and energetic signature, and the aspects or relationships they form to each other when plotted on the horoscope reveal a fascinating array of information. The birth, or Sun, sign is the sign of the zodiac that the Sun was passing through at the time of birth. The energetic signature of the Sun is concerned with a person's sense of uniqueness and self-esteem. To be a vital and creative individual is a fundamental need, and a person's Sun sign represents how that need most happily manifests in that person. This is one of the most important factors taken into account by astrologers. Each of the twelve Sun signs has a myriad of ways in which it can express its core meaning. The more a person learns about their individual Sun sign, the more they can express their own unique identity.

ZODIAC WHEEL

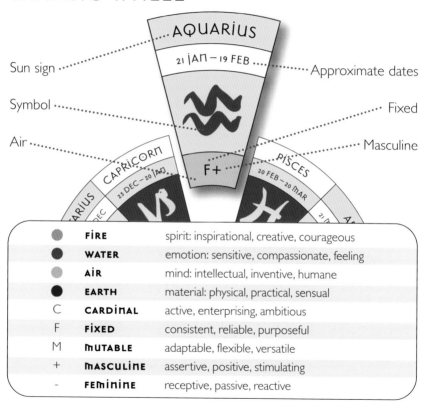

Sun sign .... AQUARIUS

Approximate dates ..... 21 JAN – 19 FEB

Symbol ....

Air ....

CAPRICORN

23 DEC – 20 JAN

PISCES

20 FEB – 20 MAR

Fixed

Masculine

F+

🔴	**FIRE**	spirit: inspirational, creative, courageous
🔴	**WATER**	emotion: sensitive, compassionate, feeling
🟡	**AIR**	mind: intellectual, inventive, humane
⚫	**EARTH**	material: physical, practical, sensual
C	**CARDINAL**	active, enterprising, ambitious
F	**FIXED**	consistent, reliable, purposeful
M	**MUTABLE**	adaptable, flexible, versatile
+	**MASCULINE**	assertive, positive, stimulating
-	**FEMININE**	receptive, passive, reactive

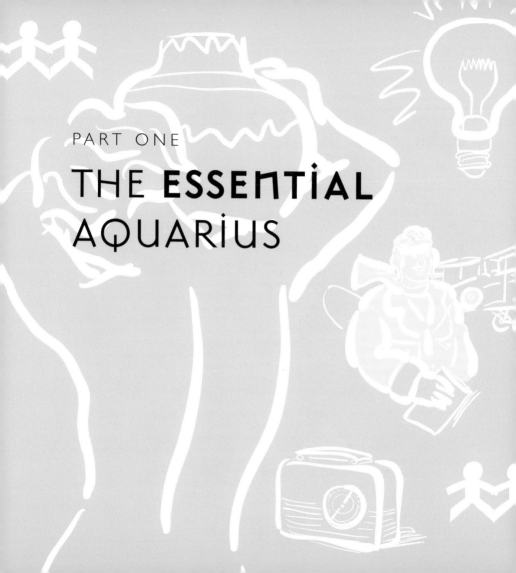

PART ONE

THE **ESSENTIAL** AQUARIUS

RULERSHİPS

Aquarius is the eleventh sign of the zodiac and the third Air sign after Gemini and Libra. It is traditionally ruled by the planet Saturn but the planet Uranus also has a close affinity with it. The symbol for Aquarius is the Water-Bearer. There are earthly correspondences of everything in life for each of the Sun signs. The part of the human body that Aquarius represents is the ankles. Aquarius is a Fixed and Masculine sign. Its gemstones are amethyst, almandine garnet, moss agate, and hematite. Aquarius signifies places that are hilly or uneven, or that are near springs, as well as vineyards and roofs of houses. It also represents dragonwort and myrrh, electricity, IT, computers, radio, and x-rays, as well as engineers, physicists, pilots, humanitarians, friends, and inventors.

AQUARIUS

The part of the human body that
Aquarius represents is the ankles.

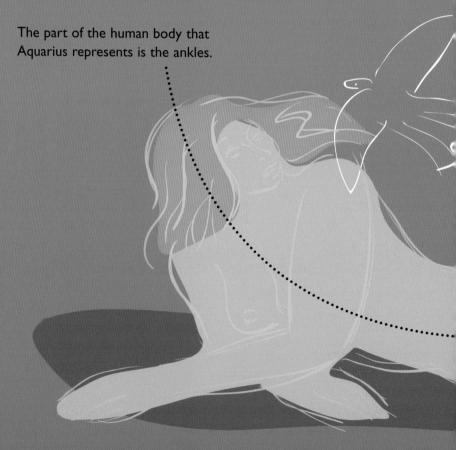

vineyards, pilots

inventors

PERSONALITY

Aquarians are thinkers—they think about ideals and, because they're rarely satisfied with the status quo, their focus is on the future. They're constantly conjuring up better ways for mankind to get along and live together in harmony. In their ideal world everyone is equal, everyone has a place, and everyone is valued. However, though they long to be included in this great extended global family, they can also be detached and removed from it on both a physical and an emotional level. This is due to their need to be free to continue with their mental questing into the realms of the new and original. It's not unusual to find some Aquarius individuals living in an ivory tower of their own making. Here they find the intellectual inspiration and insight that they bestow on humanity for the good of all. Their concern is with the group and within it they are unselfish, giving, and friendly. They will champion any worthwhile cause or underdog because they think it's only fair. And having everything fair and equal is a cause worth fighting for.

Yet Aquarius is a sign full of paradox, for although what drives Aquarians is their idealistic desire to achieve equality between all the people in a group, they also have a need to express themselves as individuals and can appreciate what distinguishes and differentiates one person from another. They themselves are unique individuals yet, at the same time, they are part of the whole.

As a Fixed sign, Aquarius is loyal and at times intransigent. When Aquarians are certain about something, they'll dig their heels in. Yet they are also unpredictable, changeable, and forward-thinking, and when they are behaving apparently contrarily and inconsistently, it is because there's a method to their madness. For example, they have little problem breaking the rules and overthrowing traditionally accepted modes of operating if they find them too restrictive or if they feel that they suppress the human spirit. Aquarians are revolutionary, rebellious, and radical, at least on a mental level, and that is the reason for their reputation as innovative, inventive, and original thinkers. Whether they work as scientists (and many of them do) or not, they are always searching for new truths that can be of benefit to others. They may come up with some pretty wacky and eccentric ideas, but without this willingness to think outside the box, the world's progress would be terribly slow.

With all their attention to humanitarian ideals and mental concepts, Aquarians may seem rather dry and sterile, but nothing could be farther from the truth. They are lively, good-hearted, and sympathetic. They enjoy the company of others and will rarely turn down an invitation to a good party or pass up an opportunity to join in some lighthearted amusement. They can become thoroughly engrossed in philosophical conversations and will discuss, debate, and argue till the cows come home and yet never tire of exploring any subject from every angle. They have an enthusiastic appreciation of music, art, and literature, and can be rather accomplished artisans in their own right, particularly when they bring their own brand of uniquely original creativity to what they are doing.

There is a touch of the wild bohemian in the Aquarius character. They love freedom of expression and have a "live and let live" attitude to life that leaves little scope for passing judgment on the personal idiosyncrasies of others. Variety is the spice of life and mediocrity in both themselves and in others is something to be avoided at all costs. Just as they prefer to display those aspects of their character that set them apart from the rest of the world, so they seek out that special spark of individuality in everyone they meet and encourage them to treasure it. Indeed, with their more outrageous ideas and their rebellious attempts to shock and stimulate people, they can go a little overboard. However, Aquarians do make genuinely supportive, honest, popular friends. They flatter others by the sincere interest they show in them and have a genuine regard for what is unique about everyone. For this reason they can count a wide array of unusual and interesting people among their friends.

Yet much as they enjoy the company of friends, they also like to be left alone. They can't bear the inane chatter or pointless conversations that they inevitably have to listen to from time to time. On these occasions, they won't hesitate to make their excuses and leave, even if it's only to go and sit in their car for an hour! It's as though they simply need to lock themselves away every once in a while to gather their thoughts, review what has been said, and sort out the outlandish ideas from the ones with genuine potential. Their minds are almost always churning. Meditation is a wonderful remedy for people with such busy minds—and no doubt Aquarians understand the scientific reasons behind its therapeutic benefits for mind, body, and spirit.

Aquarians have outgoing characters yet they can be embarrassed by displays of emotion or, heaven forbid, public displays of affection. They also find it difficult to handle other people's emotional outpourings—it would be scary if there were no end to them! However, they're not devoid of feelings themselves; after all, they're made of the same stuff as everyone else. With the Water-Bearer as their zodiacal symbol, they possess water's emotive, life-giving, spiritual qualities but they keep them contained, releasing them only when their vessel is really overflowing, and then only in the company of those with whom they feel totally at ease.

It's true that Aquarians can be a little quirky and very complex, but they are pleasant, appealing, adorable human beings who are a real joy to know and love.

CAREER & MONEY

Aquarians are capable of fitting into almost any line of work, as long as they have the freedom to utilize their forward-thinking brilliance. If they happen to work in the world of fashion, for example, they'll be the ones to develop a new cutting-edge fabric that looks like different-colored liquid metals. Or, if they're more inclined to office work, they'll be the innovative person who comes up with a clever new way to increase productivity and make everyone's jobs much easier. Because of their inventiveness, humanitarianism, and innovative thinking, there are many careers that suit Aquarians. They make great social and charity workers, astronomers and psychologists, or scientists and inventors. The electronic media, such as radio, television, computers, and the Internet are all areas of work that are suited to the Water-Bearer, and they have a particular talent for IT because they are often scientifically or mathematically minded.

They are also intuitive and have a way of being inspired by the ethereal, so in the arts they are attracted to drama and acting, poetry and painting. All in all, Aquarius is one of the most intelligent signs of the zodiac and its natives are people who are usually far ahead of their time. Whatever they do in the world it will usually be avant-garde and cutting-edge. Sometimes the world won't be ready for it, but when it catches up, it will usually find that an Aquarius paved the way.

Aquarians love to make friends with people around them at work, but that doesn't stop them from doing their job properly because they are earnest, honest individuals. Not being overly ambitious for material things, they aren't the kind of people to go for the highest wage, though a quick buck is always a temptation! They have a low boredom threshold so would find it hard to resist anything that adds a bit of zest to their lives, but before they truly find themselves, they tend to change jobs rather often. Change isn't really in their nature, but it's necessary until they finally find some occupation where they feel they belong. Once they do discover their niche, they'll stay put.

When it comes to money, they're not particularly hungry for a big pay packet. What's more important is to be doing the right type of work. They would die of boredom if they worked in a factory job but if they did happen to find themselves on a production line, sooner or later their ingenious ideas for making it run better would mean that they'd quickly be promoted to a managerial position.

Aquarians are good with money and their skills are so valuable that they can always earn a good living. Being logical, rational people, they don't have to struggle to juggle their finances; if they can afford to spend, they do, and if not, they don't. It's as simple as that. They're also sensible enough to save for the future. Though they appear to be wacky, zany people, their heads are full of common sense and always sit squarely on their shoulders.

THE AQUARiUS **CHiLD**

The little Aquarius child displays a unique individuality almost from birth. Aquarius children can be erratic in their habits. They can be completely happy to stay awake all night gazing out from their cot and making gurgling noises and then sleep all day, without causing any trouble to anyone. But once these alert, intelligent, sociable children realize that all the interesting things go on during the day, they'll settle into normal patterns of waking and sleeping. But that may well be their only concession to conformity because, without even being aware of it, Aquarius children somehow manage to behave and think differently from other children.

They're unpredictable in their likes and dislikes, one day wanting one thing while totally rejecting it the next. The parent who sees their Aquarius child totally engrossed in playing with a friend's toy might think it's a good idea to go out and purchase the same toy. The child will be appreciative, but may never show the same interest in the toy again. Aquarius children like constant stimulation and lots of playmates, but given that they're so inventive, they'll never lose their enthusiasm for making up fantastic new games and activities all on their own.

Their inquiring minds often make them good students and they enjoy learning new and interesting facts, so school rarely presents them with any problems. As they grow into adolescence, they make a concerted effort to assert their individuality and their rebellious qualities become more apparent. They may try to buck the system or question authority, which can be healthy if it's not taken too far. On the whole, these quirky, intelligent, and friendly children are very interesting, certainly companionable, and rarely ever boring to have around.

PERFECT GIFTS

The perfect Aquarius gift is one that generates conversation and will keep the recipient thinking for some time after it is opened. Air signs like questions such as "What is it?" but Aquarians are also practical, so as long as they can also see a use for the gift, they'll be happy and the gift will be a huge hit.

They love things that are innovative, modern, and cutting-edge, so when buying a gift for an Aquarius, you could perhaps go to the most popular and well-stocked computer and technology store in town and ask for the latest gizmo. Take the salesperson's advice—he or she could very well be an Aquarius too! A visit to a gadget store will probably also reap rewards. Here you might find a telescope, the latest lava lamp, a clock that projects the time on the wall, or some other wacky but useful gizmo that an Aquarius will just love. Aquarians will also be delighted by a factual book, especially a scientific one, or one on astronomy that includes a map of the stars.

Aquarius rules the ankles so Aquarius ladies will love to be given a jingling ankle bracelet. Unfortunately, ankle socks don't have the same effect, not even for a man. But overall, Aquarians appreciate any gift that has been well thought out, and when it comes from a friend, they'll be touched and will come as close to a heartfelt display of emotion as they're capable of!

FAVORITE FOODS

In matters of food and drink, it's definitely quality not quantity that counts for Aquarius. The only problem is that on those rare occasions when Aquarians do get food of a truly excellent quality, they often feel an imperative to overindulge. On the whole, though, since such quality is hard to come by and usually very expensive, they tend to stick to small amounts of very tasty dishes. For them, it's all about inspiring and satisfying their palate rather than meeting any physical need.

In fact, when they're hungry and need food just for energy, they can eat without even tasting what it is they're putting in their mouths because they'll be thinking about something else. But, if they're sitting down to a meal for pleasure, then they want their taste buds titillated with spices, their imagination inspired by exotic aromas, and their eyes excited by a beautifully presented and varied display of food. And Aquarians don't always like to stick to the accepted appropriate fare for each meal; they could happily eat salad, garlic bread, and olives for breakfast, party food for lunch, and croissants or cereal for dinner. Though they do occasionally have a sweet-tooth binge, they don't, as a rule, eat dessert.

FASHION & **STYLE**

Aquarians don't dress like anybody else. They'll never walk into a party to find that they're wearing the same outfit as another guest. They might be over- or under-dressed, but they'll usually look chic and stylish in their own inimitable way. Somehow they're able to wear the most bizarre combinations of clothes without ever looking totally ridiculous. For example, they're good at putting a businesslike tailored jacket together with a pair of hippie trousers and, by using the right accessories, will pull the whole ensemble together to make a fashion statement. Their strange outfits work, but nobody will be able to pinpoint exactly why, and if anyone else tried to carry them off, they could well look or feel silly.

Aquarians are usually trendsetters rather than fashion followers, so they'll only look through glossy fashion magazines for inspiration. They'll choose a top pictured on one page and trousers or a skirt from another, or they'll simply look for an appealing silhouette that they can achieve from their existing varied and eclectic wardrobe.

They seem to have an innate understanding of how to dress for their individual body type, accentuating the good bits and hiding the not-so-good bits. They look good in patterned fabric and can usually wear any color, but black, white, and all shades of blue—from turquoise, electric blue, and baby blue through to navy—usually look best.

IDEAL HOMES

It's not easy to list any general characteristics of the Aquarius home since Aquarius is a sign that tends to be inconsistent. One Aquarius home can look very different from another, but what they do have in common are the kind of things that Aquarians collect and have on display. Whether they live in a hovel, a hotel, or a palatial abode, the Aquarius home will be full of intriguing oddities, sometimes elegantly displayed, at other times simply lined up next to one another. Such oddities might include a miniature working model of the first steam engine, a futuristic stringed instrument, a robot that delivers drinks and sweeps the floor, or a Berber carpet hanging on the wall. Some Aquarians prefer traditional objects with modern mixed in, some prefer modern with a touch of the traditional; these Aquarians may well go for a modern, minimal style to their home.

Metal is their preferred element, so they may choose it for furniture and beds, but on the other hand, they may not! The things that are always present in their homes, however, are interesting artifacts or conversation pieces that will dazzle and fascinate their guests as much as they dazzle and fascinate their owners.

PART TWO

RISING SIGNS

WHAT IS A **RISING** SIGN?

Your rising sign is the zodiacal sign that could be seen rising on the eastern horizon at the time and place of your birth. Each sign takes about two and a half hours to rise — approximately one degree every four minutes. Because it is so fast moving, the rising sign represents a very personal part of the horoscope, so even if two people were born on the same day and year as one another, their different rising signs will make them very different people.

It is easier to understand the rising sign when the entire birth chart is seen as a circular map of the heavens. Imagine the rising sign — or ascendant — at the eastern point of the circle. Opposite is where the Sun sets — the descendant. The top of the chart is the part of the sky that is above, where the Sun reaches at midday, and the bottom of the chart is below, where the Sun would be at midnight. These four points divide the circle, or birth chart, into four. Those quadrants are then each divided into three, making a total of twelve, known as houses, each of which represents a certain aspect of life. Your rising sign corresponds to the first house and establishes which sign of the zodiac occupied each of the other eleven houses when you were born.

All of which makes people astrologically different from one another; not all Aquarians are alike! The rising sign generally indicates what a person looks like. For instance, people with Leo, the sign of kings, rising, probably walk with a noble air and find that people often treat them like royalty. Those that have Pisces rising frequently have soft and sensitive looks and they might find that people are forever pouring their hearts out to them.

The rising sign is a very important part of the entire birth chart and should be considered in combination with the Sun sign and all the other planets!

THE RISING SIGNS FOR AQUARIUS

To work out your rising sign, you need to know your exact time of birth—if hospital records aren't available, try asking your family and friends. Now turn to the charts on pages 38–43. There are three charts, covering New York, Sydney, and London, all set to Greenwich Mean Time. Choose the correct chart for your place of birth and, if necessary, add or subtract the number of hours difference from GMT (for example, Sydney is approximately ten hours ahead, so you need to subtract ten hours from your time of birth). Then use a ruler to carefully find the point where your GMT time of birth meets your date of birth—this point indicates your rising sign.

AQUARIUS WITH **ARIES** RISING

With Aries rising, Aquarians have a fire in their belly; they're real go-getters but with a style that nobody else has ever had before. These people are bona fide, one hundred percent unique individuals, and though they can in some ways be rather traditional, in others they're rebellious rule-breakers who don't care what others think. But it's difficult to predict how the traditionalist versus the revolutionary will show itself in their characters. Even at a young age, these Aquarians have a competitive streak; they simply like to have fun and see everyone else doing the same. Active and interested in everything new, they need to push the envelope, to set themselves ever-increasing challenges, and to find innovative solutions to problems. Open, enthusiastic, and friendly, they're quick to laugh and just as quick to anger, but because their lightning-fast brains are constantly alert, it's not long before their thoughts take them onward and upward. The Aquarius with Aries rising is full of life and energy, sometimes exhausting, but never failing to delight others with something wonderfully new and interesting.

AQUARIUS WITH **TAURUS** RISING

The Aquarius with Taurus rising appears to mix rigid self-control with laid-back acceptance. These individuals are calm and unshockable but extremely stubborn in their opinions about what is right or wrong. It's as if they know, from a young age, that they have a goal to reach, so they're steady climbers, but they also know just how far to go. Their attempts are always measured and they look before they leap, which is why they often reach their objective with firm assurance. They're ambitious and usually do very well in their professional life because they're motivated by a desire for luxury. Money provides them with security and status, both of which they need in order to show off their originality and creativity. Pragmatic, hardworking, and stoic in the face of adversity, they stick at things when other, less determined people would give up. If they see a worthwhile, glittering prize as the reward for their efforts, nothing will stop them. They are also very romantic people. Whether they're trying to win someone's heart or aiming for a promotion, they'll achieve success with their sincere determination.

AQUARIUS WITH **GEMINI** RISING

Chatty, witty, and clever, Aquarians with Gemini rising are lighthearted and very friendly. They never seem to run out of things to say and speak quickly in a tireless, singsong voice. But for all their seeming frivolity, they have a profound, questing mind that is open to such high levels of inspiration that they're often light-years ahead of their time. Whether they're spiritual or secular in their pursuits, they have a broad perspective on life and a talent for communicating ideas in a way that everyone can understand. Restless and inquiring, they have a thirst for new experiences and knowledge. They're also very sociable creatures and are happiest when they're learning, whether following a short course, doing a university degree, or traveling—and that could mean to a foreign country or simply another neighborhood. Their idea of relaxation involves kicking back and reading, or watching other people, but whatever they're doing, their brains are set to input mode. They also enjoy conveying information to others, and that's when their output mode comes into its own. Open, youthful, and smiling, these Aquarians possess an uplifting presence that never fails to enchant those around them.

AQUARIUS WITH **CANCER** RISING

These can be some of the most affectionate and sensitive of all Aquarians because Cancer rising adds an emotional dimension to their perception of the world. The fact that they are extremely tuned in to the atmosphere and undercurrents of each situation they find themselves in accounts for their constantly changing moods. These can swing from kind, caring, and nurturing to self-protectively aloof. They have an innate and intuitive understanding of human nature and seem to know what's going on in the psyche of almost every person they meet. They see with penetrating insight beyond the facades and masks of others, yet appear secret and mysterious themselves. Like other Aquarians, they have a natural interest in other people, but Cancer rising gives them a particularly incisive quality that they use to help others to cut through the veil hiding their egos and find their true selves. As well as assisting others on this path, Aquarians with Cancer rising use their razor-sharp perception to dig deep into their own psyches and completely transform themselves. In this way, they are able to reach their full potential and their unique, real selves can bloom in all their glory.

AQUARIUS WITH **LEO** RISING

This is the "everyman," the person that all other people can relate to. But don't tell them that because they see themselves as very special one-offs! Their warmth, generosity, and friendliness act as magnets that draw others into their sphere and keep them enthralled. These individuals are big on drama and love being in the limelight. They need an audience that appreciates their originality and their idiosyncrasies, yet paradoxically they also want to share these with the world. Being accepted into and embraced by society is very important to them, but they also want to hold onto their independence and shine out as individuals, which is something that comes naturally to them. They are quite demonstrative, generous, loving individuals who are almost always involved in a partnership, whether romantic or business, for they have a need to interact with others on an intimate level in order to understand themselves more clearly. They have a strong sense of propriety and pride gained rather early in life, as a result of which they can become unmovable in their expectations both of themselves and of others.

AQUARIUS WITH **VIRGO** RISING

♍ Fussy and fastidious yet personable and friendly, the Aquarius with Virgo rising is a highly talented and amusing conversationalist. Although these individuals can appear quite aloof, demure, or even shy, they do, in fact, long for the company of like-minded individuals with whom they can connect. They apply their quick minds and focused attention to the finer details of almost any situation, displaying remarkable perception and a keen analytical ability. But it's in the work-related areas of their life that they show inspired craftsmanship and a consummate skill for communicating complex ideas in an easily understandable form. They possess a strong work ethic and have a potential for healing, not only because of their interest in health and well-being, but also because the detachment that Aquarius bestows gives them the ability to see objectively, while the analytical skills of Virgo give them a talent for rational diagnosis. They are natural troubleshooters, whether in the realm of the human body, machines, or the environment. Give them a problem and they'll find a solution; that's their forte. As for themselves, they tend to live ordered lives with everything and everyone in its place.

AQUARiUS WiTH **LiBRA** RiSiNG

Elegance, sophistication, and a romantic, artistically inclined intellect result when Aquarius has Libra rising. These individuals can create objects and atmospheres of great beauty when they put their minds to it, for they have powerful imaginations and an idealistic way of viewing the world. They are charming, attractive people who often find themselves at the center of attention. They have a welcoming, winning smile that they use to great advantage in gathering people to their cause or bringing them around to their way of thinking. They can exercise enormous influence and power over others, but they are more motivated to make a connection via mutual love and sharing. They are cerebral individuals, but since both Aquarius and Libra are Air signs, they are also people of the heart. Their quest in life is to satisfy the longings of their heart. They have a passionate need to fully express their inner self—though this can take them many years to uncover—yet they always manage to remain warm, open, and generous.

AQUARIUS WITH **SCORPIO** RISING

It's very hard to tell what's going on in the vast mind of the Aquarius with Scorpio rising. These are passionate, creative, and compelling individuals, yet they appear aloof, self-controlled, and perhaps even a little suspicious, all of which is difficult to reconcile with their caring, sensitive, and loyal natures. They combine penetrating insight with inspired intuition, which gives the impression that they have psychic abilities and are able to read the future and other people's minds. Indeed, they may have a keen interest in the occult or an instinctive knowledge and understanding of symbolism in art and literature. They pursue their various interests with passion, and although they enjoy surrounding themselves with highly intelligent, like-minded people, they stubbornly keep their own counsel and make sure that their personal life cannot be pried into by others. When it comes to family and home, they are fiercely protective. It takes a long time for Aquarians with Scorpio rising to introduce a friend or lover to their parents. That's not because they want to make a great secret of things, but because they try, as far as possible, to keep each area of their life separate from the other.

AQUARIUS WITH **SAGITTARIUS** RISING

Breadth of vision and a philosophical turn of mind make this Aquarius even more original and inventive—if that's possible. With Sagittarius rising, the search for knowledge becomes a quest for experience and for a thorough understanding of the ways of the world in all its wondrous variety. Warm-hearted, openly friendly, and inquisitive, these individuals have a delightful way about them and although they are prone to exaggeration, they are incredibly entertaining storytellers who could turn that talent into a successful career if they wished. They tread lightly through life, full of optimism and enthusiasm, yet there's nothing lightweight about their intellectual abilities or about the scale of their concerns for humanity. They do almost nothing in half-measures but instead embrace new experiences with the verve and nerve of youth. When they throw themselves into work or pleasure, they give it all they've got. Their innate curiosity helps them to open doors that other people don't even see, yet this can also get them into trouble by giving them more responsibility than they're willing to take on! These are friendly, sociable, open-minded, and objective individuals, who are quick to form kinships with those to whom they are instinctively drawn, rather than just with blood relations.

AQUARiUS WiTH **CAPRiCORN** RiSiNG

Aloof, stern, and strictly serious when they're young, Aquarians with Capricorn rising have a wisdom beyond their years but they become more relaxed, laid-back, and seemingly youthful the older they get. They are incredibly resourceful and though they may have difficulty getting their innovative, imaginative plans off the ground at first, with time they achieve great success and have much to show for their patience, effort, and original thinking. They have a wealth of diverse talents—the description "jack-of-all-trades" comes to mind—and they are practical and highly intelligent, so they're capable of just about anything. They're also ambitious, driven individuals, who happen to be very good at earning, handling, and saving money, too. Eventually, they develop just one of their many talents and this usually gives them a very decent living so that they're capable of supporting themselves financially for the rest of their lives. These formidable creatures have a knowing look in their eye and a powerful, commanding presence, but scratch the surface, and you'll find beneath an intensely excited, positive, energetic person with a sophisticated sense of humor and a dry, ironic wit.

AQUARIUS WITH **AQUARIUS** RISING

~~~ The double Aquarius is weird, wacky, and totally unique, and
~~~ possesses an irresistible charm. These Aquarians don't pretend to be anything other than what they are—friendly humanitarians who occasionally appear to get lost thinking up new ideas to make the world a better place. In fact, they're always willing to help the underdog. They're quick to get a grip on ultra-modern devices and concepts or on any new technology; indeed, they often play a part in their development. And although they might fall over themselves in their eagerness to move about physically, their intellect is razor-sharp and it's quite impossible to trip them up intellectually. They're enthusiastic about life and about other people, have a sincere interest in getting to know others, and are always ready with a smile. Their faces shine

like the sun and there's a glowing spirit about them that fills people with hope and enthusiasm. As a result, they are often people-magnets, for others are interested in getting to know them better. Aquarians with Aquarius rising are do-gooders who possess a deep well of creative thought. They are also high achievers who are much to be admired.

AQUARIUS WITH **PISCES** RISING

This is probably the most idealistic of all the idealistic people born under the sign of Aquarius, for with Pisces rising, these individuals not only have a vision, but a vision of infinite potential. It's as though they've been inspired by the vast cosmos to see the possibilities for all humanity. Sweet-natured, kind, and gentle, they give of themselves freely and don't judge others by any yardstick other than the one that measures whether they are being true to themselves. They can be quite self-sacrificing for the good of the group and without any desire for personal reward; all they want is to see that they have had a positive effect. They can appear rather confused and confusing, but in their own minds everything makes sense and everything is connected. They have vast imaginations and the intellectual agility to move through that imagination with ease and at lightning speed. Chameleonlike, they have an uncanny ability to blend into their surroundings and can often take on the mannerisms of their associates. They are full of surprises and are often mistaken for someone else simply because of their ability to adapt and change at will. This means that they make great mimics and actors.

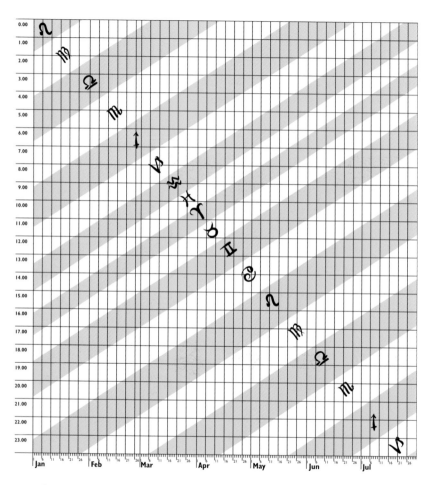

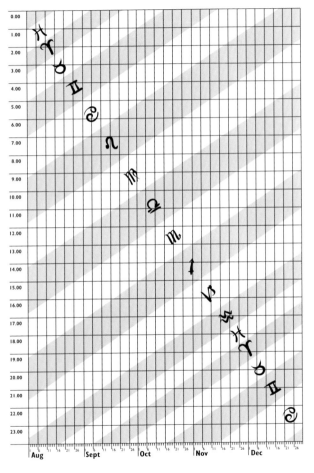

RISING SIGN
CHART

New York
latitude 39N00
meridian 75W00

♈	aries	♎	libra
♉	taurus	♏	scorpio
♊	gemini	♐	sagittarius
♋	cancer	♑	capricorn
♌	leo	♒	aquarius
♍	virgo	♓	pisces

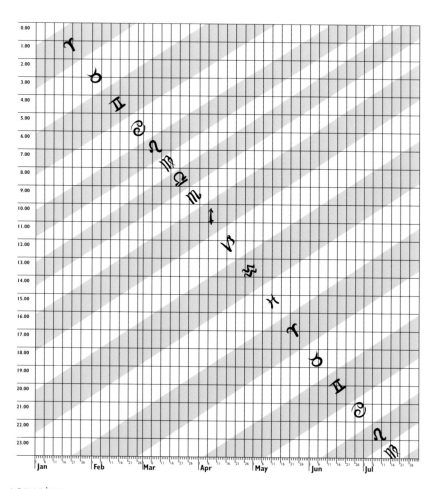

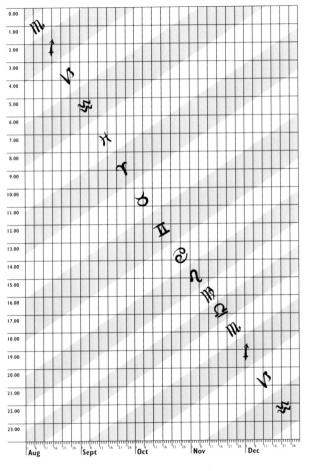

RiSiNG SiGN
CHART

Sydney
latitude 34S00
meridian 150E00

♈	aries	♎	libra
♉	taurus	♏	scorpio
♊	gemini	♐	sagittarius
♋	cancer	♑	capricorn
♌	leo	♒	aquarius
♍	virgo	♓	pisces

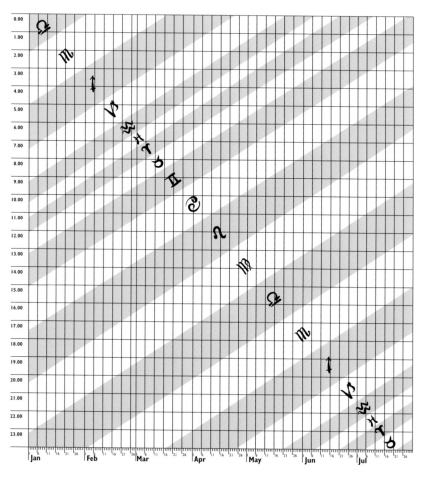

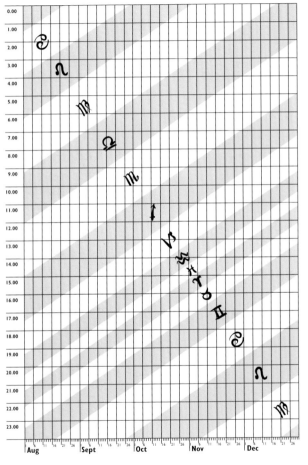

RISING SIGN
CHART

London
latitude 51N30
meridian 0W00

♈	aries	♎	libra
♉	taurus	♏	scorpio
♊	gemini	♐	sagittarius
♋	cancer	♑	capricorn
♌	leo	♒	aquarius
♍	virgo	♓	pisces

PART THREE

RELATIONSHIPS

THE AQUARIUS FRIEND

With their happy disposition and naturally sociable nature, Aquarians ethusiastically extend the hand of friendship to almost every person they meet. They're usually good fun to be around because they appreciate a laugh and a joke as well as a bit of rebellious rule-breaking.

Although they enjoy the company of large numbers of people, they can be quite exclusive about who they want to form a closer bond with, and they'll only seek further contact with people they find deeply interesting or special. However, once they've established such a bond, they'll stay loyal, supportive, and honest. Sometimes friends may wish they weren't so liberal with their honesty, but Aquarians feel that being friends gives them the right to speak their minds. After all, if they won't tell you the truth, who will?

Aquarians are also extremely fair and unbiased, which can be infuriating for anyone who expects some backup in a disagreement. However, they will certainly champion a cause they feel is worthy or, by employing their clever mental abilities, assist a friend who is being mistreated or misrepresented. In such a situation, nobody could have a better person fighting in their corner. However, they'll stop right at the point where equality has been achieved. They don't indulge in favoritism, but nor will they ever let down a friend in need—and they won't want anything in return except the gift of friendship.

AQUARIUS WITH **ARIES**

Intellectually, Aquarius stimulates and inspires Aries' hungry appetite for life. Neither of these two signs will ever be at a loss for something to do or think about. They are capable of really sparking one another off and life feels more exciting when they are in each other's company. There's an exuberant energy in a room when Aries and Aquarius are together, and they both feel very alive. However, Aquarians can be stubborn and, once decided on something, they stick to it, while Arians, infuriatingly, can get sidetracked and will move onto bigger and better things if they get the urge.

AQUARIUS WITH **TAURUS**

Aquarius is innovative and Taurus is practical and business-minded. Got the picture? As business partners, these two could end up seriously rich simply by putting their heads together. However, as friends, Aquarius might have a problem with Taurus's inability to act on the spur of the moment, and Taurus might find it hard to appreciate some of Aquarius's finer qualities, such as the love of freedom. Aquarius won't like the idea of being Taurus's best or soul—especially sole—mate. Aquarius likes to have plenty of friends. However, because both have a tendency to take up rather fixed positions, they had better enjoy getting into frequent not-so-friendly debates if this friendship is to last!

AQUARiUS WiTH GEMiNi

Aquarius and Gemini are the ultimate meeting of minds and pairing of friends. These two will have a wonderful time together, but anyone other than another Aquarius or Gemini who tries to get in on the act will feel out of place. Neither of these two deliberately choose to make anyone feel uncomfortable but their vibrational frequency is tuned to one another and to no one else. This is a friendship that could last a lifetime. They understand one another and because, for them, emotions are a foreign language, neither will let them get in the way.

AQUARiUS WiTH CANCER

When they look at each other, Aquarius and Cancer see someone very different from themselves. Aquarius loves finding out about what makes people tick, but will probably never understand the depth of emotion in Cancer. Aquarians will either stick with the friendship and try, in vain, to know Cancer better, or will meet up only occasionally because their inability to really understand Cancer will frustrate them. Cancer, on the other hand, will see where Aquarius is coming from and will really admire their humanitarian qualities, but when Aquarius is in the mood for some mental gymnastics, Cancer will simply float away.

AQUARIUS WITH **LEO**

There's an immediate sense of connection and even of fascination between Aquarius and Leo. Like all opposites of the zodiac they're on the same wavelength, so things can really buzz and zing between these two. If they find themselves in a room full of people, they'll constantly be looking to one another, not for support so much as for the shared understanding and sense of amusement that is almost telepathic between them. When they're together, it's as though they're part of a well-rehearsed double act.

AQUARIUS WITH **VIRGO**

The mental connection that these two share will allow them to enjoy hours of intellectual exploration that each will find spellbindingly stimulating. However, although mutual respect comes easily to them, a few problems could arise if Aquarius's somewhat zany ideas appear too eccentric and extreme for Virgo's final analysis. Water-Bearers want to boldly go where no mind has gone before and won't appreciate the Virgo need to ground them in reality. In short bursts, this could be a wonderfully productive duo, but coming up with ideas and plans to move forward, then stopping and starting, would be asking for trouble!

AQUARiUS WiTH **LiBRA**

This friendship is both exclusively fulfilling and widely exciting because both Aquarius and Libra are able to switch between light, frivolous banter and stratospheric intellectual idealism in the blink of an eye. They are on the same wavelength so when they head out on the town together, they make a scintillating double act that others are happy to be entertained by. But even though these two get on like a house on fire, they won't faze people who might not be up to speed with their verbal exchanges. Anyone is welcome to join their gang.

AQUARiUS WiTH **SCORPiO**

When Aquarius and Scorpio have lots of interests in common, they'll enjoy spending time in each other's company because both will respect the other's commitment and depth of understanding. Aloof but friendly, the Aquarius reluctance to get personal will suit Scorpio well, because Scorpios prefer to reveal their inner sensitivity only to their loved ones. However, if there's even the smallest note of disagreement between them, then they'll steer well clear of one another because both can be stubborn and there's a feeling between them that something nasty might erupt. In social situations they should find it easy to maintain a comfortable level of banter, as long as it's in short bursts.

AQUARIUS WITH **SAGITTARIUS**

These two have the ability to excite and inspire each other's imagination and, what's more, they'll have a good giggle at whatever those imaginations manage to concoct. They share an easy camaraderie because they accept each other at face value and wouldn't presume to pass judgment on the other. Theirs is a live-and-let-live-and-then-let's-laugh-about-it approach to life. Sagittarius's wild and wonderful streak combined with Aquarius's wacky but groovy twinkle makes a convivial combination. Combine that with the unexpected new discoveries that they make every time they meet and there's enough in it to keep them friends forever.

AQUARIUS WITH **CAPRICORN**

This can be both a frustrating and a fulfilling friendship. Aquarius loves the challenge of shocking the almost unshockable Capricorn, while the solid Capricorn is inspired and intrigued by the rebellious, wacky ideas that magically emerge from the mind of Aquarius. They both enjoy getting locked into the dry, analytical conversations that sometimes ensue from their discussions of their lofty ideals. But where Capricorns are traditional in their views and actions, Aquarians are futuristic, avant-garde thinkers. Together, these two could either inspire one another by opening doors onto new vistas of thought, or they could extinguish one another's enthusiasm entirely.

AQUARIUS WITH **AQUARIUS**

Put two Aquarius individuals in the same room and they'll be drawn together like magnets. They'll immediately commence a riveting discussion on whatever they have in common, and that will be plenty. They talk so quickly and earnestly that anyone else present would be hard-pressed to get a word in edgewise. Any such person would simply be out of sync with two Aquarians locked deep in conversation. These two totally get where the other is coming from and also appreciate each other's jokes. They often end up in fits of laughter before they've even completed a sentence because they delight in knowing where the sentence is going. In a nutshell, they get along very well.

AQUARIUS WITH **PISCES**

This is a case of two heads are better than one. There's little to disagree about when these two get together; in fact there's plenty to agree on and then develop. It would only take an evening for these two to be on track for solving the mysteries of the world. They have amazing conversations together and both have a compelling interest in what the other has to say, but just as things get rolling and Aquarius is beginning to get fascinated by it all, Pisces might start to drift off mentally to another plane. The conversation could fizzle out completely unless Pisces returns to reality pretty quickly.

THE **AQUARiUS WOMAN** iN LOVE

She can be hot, but being a creature of paradox, the Aquarius woman can be icily cold at the same time, particularly if her freedom has somehow been compromised by her man. She doesn't take to demands, and she's not the conventional kind of woman who makes sure that a hot dinner is waiting when her man comes home. She can cook, but she can't bear routine so she'll only make a meal when she feels like it—and if that happens to be in the middle of the night, so be it. The food will still be absolutely delicious.

This lady is fascinatingly unpredictable and although she doesn't appear to have any major expectations about the man in her life, she does have a few, so she'll give him the once-over long before he starts to question her suitability. Once she's satisfied with him, she'll be a very loyal lover and very trusting. Jealousy and possessiveness are alien to her; she neither understands nor tolerates them. Her intention is to enjoy life and seek out ways to improve it, not only for her own benefit, but for the benefit of all humanity. Nor is she suspicious, so just as she needs her freedom, she also gives it to her partner. The Aquarius woman won't look for trouble but if her man ever makes the grave mistake of being disloyal, he'll most definitely experience her cool side. She'll probably freeze him out of her life completely and then skip along into a more appreciative man's arms. She's never short of suitors because she has an attractively independent streak that makes a man just want to have her.

It's true that she can be emotionally aloof but she also has a huge capacity for a love that's more universal than self-centered, gushy, or romantic. However, she's not a woman who can empathize with the feelings of others for very long, especially if those feelings are hard ones. She can offer constructive, objective, no-nonsense advice but she doesn't dwell on people's woes. What would be the point? But she can be as open and demonstrative as anyone, and she'll show this side of herself more willingly if she senses that there's a clever man in the vicinity.

What turns this lady on more than anything is talk; not just any old sweet talk, but intellectually challenging conversation. She loves a man who can give as good as he gets and she's capable of carrying on a discussion way into the wee hours of the morning. The way to this woman's heart is, quite simply, through her mind—though nothing she talks about is simple. Mundane matters simply bore her but start talking quantum physics or mathematical theory and she'll be hooked. Her mind and heart will be glued not only to the conversation, but also to the clever Prince Charming who's talked his way into her life.

AQUARIUS WOMAN WITH **ARIES MAN**

In love: From the moment the gaze of the Aquarius woman falls on the Aries man, she wants him. She's intuitive about these things and while it's actually rare for an Aquarius woman to be deliberately seductive, in this case, the Aries man brings it out in her and she'll make the most of it. His energy is addictive and hers will simply electrify him. Both have an insatiable curiosity about one another and will not stop in their quest to completely uncover the other's mystique, which, of course, they'll never fully be able to do, so the curiosity just goes on and on and on. In the simplest terms, the combination of Aries man and Aquarius woman is magnetic. There's a huge charge between them that's almost tangible and that can draw them right into one another, for good. Prying them apart would be too big a challenge for any interfering female, so she shouldn't even try. But another possibility is that the high-voltage energy between the Aries man and the Aquarius woman can sometimes result in furious anger, which seems to blow up out of nowhere and which isn't fun for either of them. There is a slight possibility that this relationship could burn itself up, but the pros vastly outweigh the cons, so it's certainly worth taking the risk. This relationship has all the ingredients for a grand passion. There's nothing small about this love, and big love just grows and grows. Before they know it, they'll be an item.

In bed: This truly is a beautifully honest and sexually energetic combination. The Aquarius woman loves the way that she can have her Aries man hungry with desire and ready for some bed action whenever she wants. It's like having a man permanently at her disposal: all she has to do is say "now." He's not only happy to oblige — he can't wait. The Aries man and Aquarius woman are fast, furious, and frequent visitors to the bedroom. And that's not the only place they'll get it on; these two are innovative and kinky. It would have been a couple like Aries man and Aquarius woman who first did it in an airplane or first used sex toys. But whether they are home alone or out on the town, she won't be able to stop herself from reaching for him and he for her. He loves the spontaneity of it all and the possibility of being seen will challenge his daring and perhaps bring out his more dastardly side. All of which will, of course, really turn on that Aquarius woman. They'll both get so excited at the sheer audacity of being naughty that they might decide to try doing it in broad daylight in public. Hopefully not, however. As they're both thinkers, they'll realize that this will mean trouble and probably an end to their animal antics.

AQUARIUS WOMAN WITH **TAURUS MAN**

In love: Both the Aquarius woman and the Taurus man are rather stubborn and opinionated, so sometimes it can be fun for them to find someone to flex their muscles against. The Taurus man generally knows what he's talking about because it takes him some time to form an opinion and this appeals to the Aquarius woman because she likes a lover who she can learn new things from. However, as she also likes to think around corners, it will be very difficult for her to get her stubborn Taurus man to go along with some of her more zany ideas. He is very conservative, whereas she is original and totally idiosyncratic. She will want to smash through convention, while he feels safe playing by the rules. It is possible that these two could fall in love with each other, but it might feel as if they've done it against their better judgment. Love is not free and easy for an Aquarius woman with a Taurus man; it's more like hard work. But then again, once they've tasted the pleasures that each has to offer, coming apart may prove to be even harder work! The Aquarius lady could intellectualize for hours on end about whether to stay together or not, and certainly the Taurus man could listen. In the end, they might decide that it's simply easier to stay together and enjoy the love they have! But whatever they decide, whether together or apart, this is a relationship with impact. They won't ever forget one another.

 In bed: These two can be very sexy together. At first, the Aquarius woman enjoys the experience of getting to know what "does it" for her Taurus man. She absolutely adores experimenting and trying out new things, and she'll want to please this man because he's so deliciously happy when he's making love. He is so fascinated by her electric response to his touch that he just wants to touch her over and over again. However, what she responds to one minute doesn't necessarily do it for her the next. Variety is a spice of her life, but it can be variety within just one relationship, so long as that relationship is flexible enough. In the long run, the Lady Water-Bearer could be too physically aloof for her Bull lover, and far too unpredictable. One day she is compellingly committed to engaging in erotic pleasure and the next, faced with her Taurus lover panting and reaching out to her from the bed, she'll assume that he's injured himself and simply wants help getting up. This kind of behavior has a very destabilizing effect on the sensitive male ego of the physically demanding Taurus man; he just can't understand how she can be so inconstant in her desires. He knows that she's not frigid and he's well aware of how passionate she can be, yet sometimes she seems so cold. He needs lots of affection; she needs lots of variety. The sex may become so predictable that she ends up lying back thinking about the shopping list while he lies on top getting on with the job.

AQUARIUS WOMAN WITH GEMINI MAN

In love: What a delightful couple the Gemini man and Aquarius woman make. They say that "time flies when you're having fun." If that's the case, then these two will certainly be old and gray before they know it! Life for them will just hurtle along at a breathtaking pace in an exciting blur of love and laughter. They'll spend many a night chatting and chirping away like a couple of lovebirds in spring. But it won't all be lightweight, frivolous banter; these two will get into such seemingly way-out, seriously mind-expanding, philosophical discussions that they'll believe they're the first ever to travel this intellectual terrain. Although they can be very much in love, they would never be seen canoodling in the corner of a subway car or on a bus. They're far too busy chatting away. Both are capable of writing beautiful romantic poetry and they often do, even in the little notes and text messages they send to one another. Theirs is the kind of love that doesn't need constant demonstration. The only problem that could undermine this near-perfect relationship is that the Gemini man can be evasive and the Aquarius woman can be detached. This makes developing the relationship into something more than friendship a little hit-or-miss in the early stages, but once they fall in love, they'll realize what a valuable commodity they possess, and with all their fun and laughter, they'll be rich beyond measure.

In bed: Physical love between a Gemini man and an Aquarius woman is a breathtaking experience—full of surprise and wonder. She has a few tricks up her sleeve, not least because she's amazingly inventive and can be relied upon to come up with some very original ways of capturing the Gemini man's attention. She's quite unlike anyone he's known before. Some would say that she's a kinky kind of lover. With her alternative spin on every possible position, her antics will definitely fire him up! She'll be his ultimate spine-tingling experience, and she'll love how he loves it. He's a playful lover so she should feel no embarrassment in getting out the toys. If she hasn't already acquired any, then a trip to the toy store will be a stimulating and hilariously sexy outing for them both. They make a great team; the Aquarius woman's very definitely his match in the game of verbal foreplay. When these two jump into bed together there's a mutual feeling that here is someone with whom they can be truly free. Their sexual prowess is not going to be marked on any score card, so they can abandon any hang-ups or performance anxiety they might have. The result is truly fantastic and sensually thrilling!

AQUARIUS WOMAN WITH **CANCER MAN**

 In love: The attraction between these two lies in the fact that both are fascinated by the strange, abstract, and mystical side of life and both find the other strange, abstract, and mystical, too! The sweet Cancer man will pull hard at the alluring Aquarius lady's heartstrings, which will not be a comfortable experience for her. She prefers discretion and friendship, and though she likes to talk, she prefers, if at all possible, not to talk about personal feelings. He'll find her aloof sophistication an irresistible challenge and will do his utmost to extract an emotional response from her. If none is forthcoming he'll feel crushed and then he'll tell her that it's all her fault! She won't be able to see why she should take the blame when she's done nothing wrong … and so it goes on. The Cancer man is all about emotional attachment, while she prefers emotional detachment. She may find him deliciously interesting and extremely attractive, but keeping him happy could be too much like hard work. One thing that fills her with fear is his possessiveness and his need for nurturing; the Aquarius girl isn't against commitment, it's simply that she's too involved with humanity as a whole to focus all her care and attention on just one person. It won't be easy for them to find a middle ground, but never say never. Even if it doesn't happen in this space–time continuum, there's always a chance that these two will find their way together to heaven and beyond!

In bed: The Aquarius girl has an unconventional approach to sex so she won't get off on romance and tenderness. The first time she hears those sweet violins while the romantic Cancer man is kissing and caressing her, she'll no doubt feel shivers all over. But by the second, let alone the twentieth time, her eyes will probably wander to the clock and she'll be wondering what time her friends are meeting up. He wants to feel loved and nurtured, and needs to develop a deep emotional bond in order to get his sexuality pumping, while she likes a bit of unpredictability and some shock tactics. She'd really love her Cancer man to be spontaneous, show up when she's out meeting up with her pals, and pounce on her. He, of course, would feel totally adored if she blew going out with her friends and instead stayed home and let her gentle airy breeze blow over him. These two just don't get where the other's coming from. He would take it as a personal insult to his prowess if she ever suggested something a little kinky, even just rock music instead of the violins.

AQUARIUS WOMAN WITH **LEO MAN**

 In love: Only the Lion could make a Water-Bearer feel so passionate about a relationship and the fact that they are opposites in the zodiac simply intensifies the attraction. Her aloof but friendly manner appeals to him because he admires her independence and individuality, and he will be flattered when his efforts to gain her attention result in her showing a sincere and sparkling interest in him. And she'll be very interested in him indeed; in fact she'll be extremely appreciative of all his extravagance, glamour, and showy exhibitionism. There's just a touch of elitism about the Aquarius woman, so haughty Leo's natural nobility and exclusivity really do it for her, while he loves the fact that she's totally unique and different from the common crowd. His pride gets a boost when he's seen with a woman who has such an electrifying effect on others. In fact, they both take pride in one another. She inflates his ego and self-confidence so much that when she's not around he often feels flat, but sometimes her impartiality and dislike for the green-eyed monster wound Mr. Leo because he needs to be the center of her world. It would serve them well to remember that they are both very loyal creatures, who want only the best for one another and the chance to express their love freely. Whenever the world tries to encroach on these two lovers, they activate their exclusive magnetic vibrations, sticking together so tightly that nothing and no one can come between them.

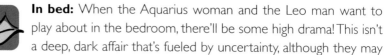

In bed: When the Aquarius woman and the Leo man want to play about in the bedroom, there'll be some high drama! This isn't a deep, dark affair that's fueled by uncertainty, although they may want to play it that way. It's apparent from the playful, twinkling look in their eyes that they'll be laughing all the way and having lots of fun together. The Leo man is a performer, no doubt about it, and because he's so generous she only needs to let him know what deeds she wants performed, and he'll rise to the occasion. She's an extremely innovative lover with plenty of shocking surprises that will delight and excite him. He's pretty creative himself, and his wild, flamboyant displays of passion will encourage her to show just how inventive and original she can be. Both of them could get into a little friendly competition, showing off their individual talents. They may, after a while, find it a little difficult to keep up this buzzing frequency of sexual excitement but, since he's so playful and she's not unfamiliar with the joys of toys, their bedroom games will continue to have an electrifying quality. Even when the Lion is feeling languorous and lazy, she'll still be able to arouse his interest by stroking him with exotic massage oils and willl soon have him purring like a pussycat.

AQUARIUS WOMAN WITH VIRGO MAN

In love: This is a meeting of minds, with both openly admiring the other for their amicability, intelligence, and communication skills. It's likely to be the combination of the inventive ideas of the

Aquarius woman and the detailed elaborations of the Virgo man that brings them together and has them spending night after night indulging in exciting philosophical and psychological conversations. The constant reshaping of their thoughts will keep them together for some time but theirs is unlikely to be a great romance or a grand passion. It's more likely to be a solid friendship, since intelligent conversation is important to both. They'll get plenty out of it when they're together, but it won't be easy for either to commit to this relationship because both remain a little aloof from expressing their emotions. Love can grow between them even though it may never really be earth-shattering. They may feel that there must be something more, which is sad as they've come so far; the compatibility is there and that's not an easy thing to find. She might not like it when he gets picky because that draws her down avenues of thought where she doesn't want to go, and the same will be true for him when she comes up with some of her more eccentric ideas. They'll be friends forever; both are so easygoing that they just can't help but like each other enormously, but love? Well, that may be a tall order unless there's some deeper connection.

In bed: The foreplay of these two will be truly fantastic. With their sexy verbal banter both have a way of winding the other up into a state of expectation and excitement. They'll find it teasing and tantalizing to imagine the sexual talents that the other possesses and they can really get each other into a frenzy of jittery anticipation, but somehow, the idea of sex together is so much better than the reality. If the Aquarius woman spends too long with the Virgo man as her lover, she might begin to climb the walls in frustration. She's naturally very loyal but variety is the spice of her life and although he's rather versatile, his efficiency will eventually become too predictable for her. Meanwhile, the Virgo man can pick up a complex quicker than he can catch a cold and unless she knows how to build up his ego, he might just whimper and run away, which is not what she wants. He deserves more and so does she. It can work between them but they both need to make a conscious effort to tune in to each other and to stay that way. They're both so cool that they need to work at raising the sensual heat above tepid.

AQUARIUS WOMAN WITH **LIBRA MAN**

 In love: There's a chemistry here that's hard to ignore. Although the Aquarius woman isn't overly romantic and actually feels rather uncomfortable with the compliments, flowers, and other love tokens that are Mr. Libra's stock-in-trade, when he has her in his sights, this is a beautiful relationship. His way of expressing love is light and breezy, and expands her view of what love is all about. She also finds it refreshing because it doesn't come with any strings attached. He'll captivate her so gently that she won't even notice it and no one else is as capable as he is of bringing out so sweetly and completely the soft, ladylike femininity of an Aquarius woman. Her original, entertaining conversation inspires him to think in idealistic terms and she shows him how creative his fantasies could be with a little help from her. This is a love that starts in the mind, then moves into the heart. There will rarely be any unpleasant scenes or harsh words between them, just a natural inclination to see the best in each other. However, if at times the Libra man's feeling off balance because of her lack of attachment, the only way he can right himself is to put her off balance, too, but she'll usually be able to cope pretty well with that. Life and love flow easily between these two, and as long as they can keep their flirty eyes from wandering, theirs should be a long-lived love affair.

 In bed: Sex between a Libra man and Aquarius woman is like a flight of fancy that's fueled by words of encouragement. He gets incredibly turned on by her bedroom banter because she speaks the unspeakable in the most gentle and seductive tones and when she tells him he's gorgeous, he'll devote hours to her pleasure and enjoyment. He also loves it when she dresses up, so she could slip into her white, silky lingerie and then, when she's done that, if he hasn't seen to it first, she could light some scented candles and whisper even more sweet, sensual nothings in his ear. He appreciates her inventive sexual storytelling more than most and gets excited by her original, erotic fantasies. He's spent so much time thinking about the most wonderful and perfect ways to do "it" that he finds it quite a turn-on to have someone come up with kinky new ideas that even he hasn't thought of. She, meanwhile, will be drawn in by the romantic wonder with which he expresses his love and need for her. That will push back even farther the boundaries of her vast imagination and will inspire her to do things for him that will make the hairs on his chest stand up on end! Lovemaking between these two is smooth and sensual, and loving, yet light as air. This girl's famous for being detached but with a Libra man she can get very attached indeed.

AQUARIUS WOMAN WITH **SCORPIO MAN**

 In love: Initially, the attraction between an Aquarius lady and a Scorpio man is strong; both like to get into people's heads and find out what makes them tick and once they discover a little more about one another, they'll be even more intrigued. But when the Aquarius lady comes up against all that dark, brooding intensity in the Scorpio man, she'll want to shy away, and in most cases that would be the thing to do. But if she likes to live dangerously, then he's the man for her. Their deep understanding of the mysteries of life and their fascination with things spiritual give them some common ground on which to start building their love. At times, however, stubbornness on both sides could result in an impasse. To top that, he's very possessive and jealous, and that sort of thing simply makes Aquarius retreat. She's naturally independent and won't make it easy for the Scorpio man to weave those bonds of emotional intimacy that have to be firmly in place for him before he'll expose that side of his nature that she'd find so precious and endearing. She's unlikely to have the tolerance or emotional sensitivity to see anything other than the negative side of his romantic character. There's potential here, but with all the angst that develops from their differences, would either of them really want it to last forever? They'd have to be gluttons for punishment, and if they are, there would need to be another factor to seductively bind them together. And so to bed…

In bed: The Scorpio man's fierce passion is very thrilling and sexy, but his emotions could be a little overpowering for the cool Aquarius woman. She rather likes the idea of this sexual relationship and delights in sharing her fantasies with him until he turns to steam and is carried ever upward by her sexy words. But the reality of totally merging with him at such a high level might not be so wonderful for her! This relationship could simply be too stormy, and although the electricity it generates is exhilarating, when he gathers himself into an ominous dark cloud, the threat of a driving rain of emotion makes her shiver, and not perhaps in the way he'd hope! She's very attracted to pleasure and amusements, and he'll offer her just about the best ride in the fair—an eye popping, breathtaking, white-knuckle ride that's so moving, she won't know whether to laugh or cry when it comes to a stop. There's an element of competition between these two so they could well fight for control, for instance, to see who gets to tie whom to the bedposts. This sort of tussle is fun for a while, particularly for the Scorpio man, who likes to have a spirited lady in his bed, but in the long run, unless she's willing to submit to him, she might feel that burning sting of his Scorpion's tail. And when that happens, it stops being amusing; the whole thing could get too dark and scary for her to deal with.

AQUARIUS WOMAN WITH **SAGITTARIUS MAN**

In love: There's nothing and no one quite like a Sagittarius man for capturing the heart and imagination of an Aquarius woman. His free-spirited approach to life is like a breath of fresh air that carries her along on an exciting adventure, while she's everything that he loves in a woman—independent, intelligent, gregarious, and with a unique, nonchalant sex appeal that arouses his longing to know more about her. It just feels so right and easy between them and they bring out the best in each other. They automatically allow each other the space they need to reach their full potential, leaving plenty of room for an honest love to blossom between them. What could possibly go wrong? Well, there's a slight chance that, because they're both out discovering things or saving the world, finding time to be together might prove difficult. The good thing is that the Aquarius woman is about as reasonable as they come and the Sagittarius man will forever fascinate and stimulate her inquiring mind. So long as they keep the channels of communication open and intimacy high on their list of priorities, there'll be no end to their delight in one another. Neither will try to hold the other back; instead they'll nurture each other's aims and ideals. They value the mutual attraction, friendship, and honesty that they share, as well as those frequent occasions when their laughter at the absurdities of life and at each other brings them close. This one is for keeps. This couple born of Fire and Air get on like a house on fire.

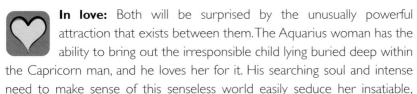

In bed: This is one hot-to-trot relationship! The Aquarius woman is as innovative and inventive as the Sagittatrius man is lusty and adventurous, so when these two are together, things can get pretty wild. Spontaneity is the name of the game between these two lovers and it's a game that they both want to play. The Sagittarius man and the Aquarius woman could find themselves swinging from the chandelier one minute and sweating over the stove the next. This couple is really cooking and they serve up something very tasty indeed! Any place, any time— morning, noon, or night—and anything and everything goes. The Sagittarius/Aquarius sex life is pure passion. There may be the odd occasion when she needs more foreplay, both verbal and physical, for he has a tendency to silently and stealthily get her in his sights then unexpectedly pierce her with his Archer's arrow, but since there'll definitely be many erotic replays, she'll soon learn to read the signs and be alert to his huntsman's tactics. And she may well use her imagination to reverse the predator-prey roles and lead him on a merry chase around the bedroom!

AQUARİUS WOMAN WİTH **CAPRİCORN MAN**

In love: Both will be surprised by the unusually powerful attraction that exists between them. The Aquarius woman has the ability to bring out the irresponsible child lying buried deep within the Capricorn man, and he loves her for it. His searching soul and intense need to make sense of this senseless world easily seduce her insatiable, inquiring mind. Both have a broad vision, and their inexhaustibly long conversations that take place into the wee hours of the night have a wonderful way of turning fantasy into reality. If they never slept, they'd probably solve all the problems of the world in one extended sitting, but they'd always be interrupted by the need to delve deeply into each other's physicality. However, the Aquarius girl may sometimes find it difficult to meet his demands for a more intense expression of love, which doesn't come easily to her. She'll suppress her emotional reactions until she can express them verbally. At times, she'll feel the urge to rebel against his stern traditionalism and will demonstrate her love in such an original way that he either won't get it at all or won't like it. He may think that by providing her with material comfort and physical attention he has the right to some control over her life, but she's too independent to allow that. At the end of it all, both are realistic enough to recognize that their differences could enhance their relationship, but they'll also know whether, in this case, there are simply too many differences for it to succeed.

 In bed: He's sexy, insatiable, and intense. The Capricorn man is a horny old Goat no matter what his age, and for the experimental Aquarius woman that's a real turn-on. She'll certainly want to try him on for size and to try out some of her own new tricks and turns, too. She'll have a bit of a surprise with this randy Goat, though, because until she gets naked with him, his sober appearance won't give away his deep eroticism. He'll be right in there with her, and he's got the stamina and patience to put up with her endless experimentation. Thankfully, she's a quick study and because he likes all forms of physical loving, even her more wacky ideas will simply fill him with amusement and a willingness to indulge her. But where she can get off on sexual fantasy, his needs are all down and dirty. When they're not together, this guy won't be satisfied by late-night phone sex; he wants her there next to him. If she ever planned to turn him on this way, then she should think again, because the moment she hangs up the phone, he'll be grabbing his address book and reaching for his coat to go in search of a flesh-and-blood lover. When their moods coincide then the peaks of pleasure they can reach are limitless, but when they don't, it all feels like a lead balloon. This coupling is sometimes so right and sometimes so not. Either way, they'll both be in for an unforgettable ride.

AQUARiUS WOMAN WiTH **AQUARiUS MAN**

In love: The only person who isn't mystified by Aquarius is another Aquarius; they understand each other so well. When they're in love, romance isn't high on the agenda but there's a charmingly naive quality about the way they express their feelings, while the scintillating conversations they share go a long way toward forming a deep, loving bond between them. With these two there'll be no getting bogged down in clinging, clawing emotion; they're simply two terrific friends who also happen to be in love. And since friendship is the basis for their relationship, even when they aren't feeling that amorous toward each other, they can still enjoy sincere companionship, laughter, and amusement. Liking each other is somehow more important to these two than loving each other; obsessive, passionate, love–hate styles of relating don't make sense to them at all. They accept each other's need to feel independent, free, and supported in their individuality. However, if there's to be one sticking point, it's that both can be a bit rigid in their expectations of the other's role in the relationship, and either one or both of them will turn very cool if those expectations aren't being met. They don't necessarily speak about what's going on in their inner worlds, but if they were occasionally to talk about their hopes and fears for the relationship, as well as having gripping cosmic conversations about the wonders of the outside world, then this could be a long-lasting partnership.

In bed: For the Aquarius man and woman, it's all about quality not quantity. They might end up going for days or weeks without sex, then do nothing for a fortnight but indulge in some serious nooky. And no, they don't tire of one another, because between them they can find at least one thousand and one different ways of doing it. Erotic ideas flow from them like the Trevi Fountain; no one but a fellow Aquarius could imagine what's possible for two people to do in the pursuit of sexual stimulation. Since they make love with their minds, foreplay is often verbal; they turn each other on by fantasizing aloud and with such detachment that the need to become physically attached becomes even greater. Aquarians might not have the sexual confidence of some of the other signs, but what they lack in self-assurance they more than make up for in originality. Sex between two Water-Bearers is funky, different, wild, and totally spontaneous, and when they put their inventive minds together, they could end up doing it anywhere or anyhow. They'll certainly try anything once—particularly anything involving multiples—and if it doesn't do any harm, they'll probably try it again some time! Trust is rarely an issue between them because they know where they stand with each other. And when they're in physical proximity, then they're together, and no one can come between them.

AQUARIUS WOMAN WITH PISCES MAN

In love: The Pisces man will fascinate the Aquarius woman in the most hypnotic way and she will appeal to his desire for something beyond the here and now. Unlike many women, she understands the Pisces man, that is until he begins to talk about emotions. He'll have to trust his instincts when it comes to her emotional commitment because she may sound a little dry and analytical whenever he attempts to immerse her in conversation about it. She'll simply switch off or go off on a different intellectual tangent but, luckily, he'll just start thinking about whatever it is she's talking about. He's intuitive and empathetic, so he's capable of following her intellectual lead. He'll blend into her and she'll encourage his individuality, so they can be very good for one another. These two will be so impressed with each other on a mental and a spiritual level, that it may take the Aquarius woman a long time to realize that, beneath the surface, her Pisces lover is a very sensitive man. Similarly, he won't initially recognize her need for independence. By this point they may already be in love—which amounts to commitment—though she may find it difficult to verbalize it. She may be too detached for him; his insecurities need a lot of emotional support, and this doesn't come naturally to the Aquarius girl. However, with a little work and a lot of love, these two could end up as a very heavenly match.

 In bed: For this couple, sex will rarely start in bed. It's more likely to begin when they're out doing something else, like the grocery shopping, and if they find any opportunities for double entendres, then the jokes will start. They'll carry on all the way home until, as they come through the door, they can hardly keep their hands off one another. When Lady Aquarius finally slides into bed with her horny Pisces man, she'll realize that this is an experience that will take her over the edge and beyond. And he won't stop at the usual boundaries of erotic togetherness so she could find herself floating off into a fantasy land, where she loses touch with her body and with what's happening on the physical plane. He knows instinctively that she's a lover who's capable of stratospheric levels of pleasure and he knows how to release her inner sex goddess. That all sounds very lovely, but then she comes down to earth with a bump. Never mind. There's definitely more to this couple than just being in bed together. They're making love all the time, whether it's with sassy, saucy suggestions over the phone, or by making dirty bedroom eyes at one another across the table at a dinner party. The best thing is that they always live up to their promises and take those promises all the way.

THE **AQUARiUS MAN** iN LOVE

Love is a very strange concept for the Aquarius man. He doesn't quite know how to express it in a way that other people or, most particularly, his lover, can easily interpret. But he completely understands infatuation and rather frequently, too, because he finds that interesting, attractive women arouse his romantic fascination all the time—and he meets so many of them! But he's quite discerning and knows how quickly he can become disenchanted or bored if there isn't some intriguing quality to keep his attention. The excitement of his amorous intentions very quickly dries up when the ordinary and predictable start to feature regularly in his relationships.

Once he sets eyes on someone special and picks up signals that the interest is mutual, then he'll do everything in his power to put himself in their line of sight so he can show off his qualities. He's not the caveman type who will hit a woman over the head and drag her off to be his mate. His methods of seduction are much more refined and a whole lot less obvious. He'll dazzle with his intellect, inspire with his imagination, and show his appreciation with a detached but lively sense of fun and respect. In fact, he's very good at pretending that he's not interested in pursuing a romantic liaison at all, and that the only reason he wants to develop a relationship is for camaraderie and friendship. And that actually isn't so far from the truth. For the Aquarius man to be really in love, he needs to feel that he has a potential companion for life at his side and that he can count his partner as the best among his many friends.

Intimacy for him is established in the mind, so if he and his lover don't share the same interests and ideals, then he's unlikely to find the relationship very fulfilling. Although he can feel as deeply as any other person, it's the expression of those emotions that he finds so difficult, and he also finds it difficult when his lover expresses hers. It's often beyond him to display irrational feelings and vulnerability, but unless he can put it all into words, there may be no indication that he does, indeed, have a loyal, loving, and passionate heart. He'll rarely display jealousy or anger, no matter how much he feels them inside; he'll suppress any hurt and confusion rather than lose control of the rational demeanor he shows to the world. Any attempt to drag a reaction out of him will be met with cool disdain and he'll retreat behind a wall of aloof nonchalance.

This guy doesn't fit the mold of sensitive, romantic hero, but he's honest, sincere, and so fascinating that if he's allowed to express his love through friendship, he's capable of capturing the heart of many a fair maiden— though just one will usually do.

AQUARIUS MAN WITH **ARIES WOMAN**

 In love: The gregarious Aquarius man and the expressive Aries woman make for a great combination. She loves him for the way he continually comes up with fascinating facts and original ideas. He adores her independence and willingness to try anything new. They'll both be stimulated by the ever-moving flow of thought, inspiration, and information between them. They'll feed off each other and would do so literally, given the chance, but there's just one thing that might make it difficult for this relationship to move beyond devoted friendship. He appears emotionally aloof. Even if he can't get her out of his mind, the Aquarius man has a very hard time letting the Aries woman know just how deeply she affects him. He'll be lapping up her direct and ardent expressions of love, yet somehow he can't quite make the leap and declare his feelings with the same amount of fervor. He'll call her up, ask her to meet him, take her to dinner, and generally try to spend as much time in her company as possible, but he needs to be completely sure that he won't be rejected before he lets her see into his heart and the enormous amount of space she takes up there. Luckily, most Aries girls have good instincts, so she'll know without having to be told. This relationship is in no way hard work for either of them. In fact, there's no need to try at all; there is a natural love and acceptance between them, and neither will ever feel bored!

In bed: The Aquarius man is an innovative lover. Even a thrill-seeking Aries woman will be left with dropped jaw and raised eyebrows at some of his sexual suggestions. He'll love the fact that she'll never say no, and why would she? His perceptive friendliness along with his inventive and occasionally kinky sexuality makes him her ultimate turn-on. Intellectually, this man stimulates and inspires the hungry Aries woman's appetite for life, so she'll never fret for something to do or think about, in or out of bed. Her quick and agile mind ensures that he'll never be bored as long as his attention is centered on her. She is youthful, active, and equally inspiring to him, which helps to shake his detached demeanor into something that could look suspiciously like intimacy. They offer one another the freedom they both need but one great thing about the sexual relationship of an Aquarius man and an Aries woman is their total lack of inhibition. When both are satisfied, they'll happily lie around talking about some fascinating subject until the glow of dawn creeps in through the window then, rather than roll over and go to sleep, they'll be rested enough to make love all over again and until well past breakfast.

AQUARIUS MAN WITH **TAURUS WOMAN**

In love: There are occasions when the Taurus lady will find interests in common with the Aquarius man, for instance, a mutual love and admiration for what the other is capable of. With his perceptive and friendly nature, the Aquarius man has much to offer her, especially in the way of keeping her up-to-date with modern thoughts and trends. However, his allergic reaction to anything remotely emotional and sentimental could bring this romantic and sensitive girl out in a bad case of weeping heart. For much as he adores her luxurious femininity and depth of understanding, even she will be hard-pressed to understand the manner in which he expresses it. The Aquarius man is detached from his emotions, although he often doesn't realize it. He is an admirable humanitarian at heart, but often forgets to nurture and adore those who are closest to him, while the Taurus woman will nurture and adore him and won't be able to comprehend why he doesn't return the compliment. If the Taurus woman can manage to find her own inner security while also cherishing the innumerable qualities of the Aquarius man, and if he can realize how good he feels bathed in her love and warmth, then he might just budge from his non-committal stance. This relationship grows slowly, but if the initial attraction retains a touch of sweetness, then it shouldn't be given up on too soon, though it will probably go through some bitter moments before it matures and ripens into a delicious, fruitful partnership.

In bed: Everyone's got a bend, one way or another, but the Aquarius man is downright kinky; there isn't a sexual position in the book that he hasn't tried, although it would be fun to challenge him! That would certainly keep him interested, which is exactly what the Taurus lady needs to do if he is to indulge her desire for sensual fulfilment. However, if she has it her way, he'll occasionally need to stop intellectualizing and trying to figure out the latest Kama Sutra contortion, and will simply have to indulge in the physical process. Whether it's his way or her way, the delightful result will be that they're trying something new all the time. If she draws on her resources of patience, she'll get her fair share of bliss, but he'll probably have to struggle to maintain his need for innovation and she may be frustrated in her desire for emotional connection through lovemaking. Emotions get in the way of what he sees as the true meaning of love, so she could spend all evening listening to him discussing the abstract causes of love, rather than getting down to it. Sex is not the way to this man's heart. It's only the way into his trousers. He doesn't need physical affection to make him feel loved and wanted the way a Taurus girl does.

AQUARIUS MAN WITH GEMINI WOMAN

In love: The blend of Gemini woman with Aquarius man puts them on a learning curve, but it's not like they're back at school in the dreary classrooms of their youth. It's more like they're studying in the University of Life's Quirky Department of the Weird and Wonderful. These two together create a bubble of exclusivity whose rules only they understand. It floats about on the wind and through it they view the world from a unique and fascinating perspective. Both of them loathe the ordinary and the mundane and they are permanently on a mission to seek out the unusual and the exciting. Each is fond of the knowledge and information that the other imparts. They inspire each other to explore new areas of contemplation and, what's more, they laugh together on a regular basis. The Aquarius man adores being in the position of teaching the more scatterbrained Gemini girl how to organize her life by using the latest cutting-edge technology, and she simply loves it that he understands and supports her constant need for change and growth. They have their own brand of romance that suits them perfectly; it's neither gushy nor emotional, and it gives them a smooth flight without any extreme highs or lows. There isn't a "falling-in-love" stage for these two; they love each other naturally when they first meet, whether that's as friends or as potential dates. On some level, both sense that they are birds of a feather and since both are born under the element of Air, they could flock together for life.

In bed: The Aquarius man and Gemini woman never run the risk of becoming bored when it comes to sex. Because they have so much in common, they feel as if they've known each other for a lifetime so they trust one another when it comes to experimentation. And experimentation rules with them, so anyone who thinks they're the first to try it in a particular place or position will probably find that the Aquarius man and Gemini woman have already tried it. This couple are founding members of the Mile-High Club, yet that's not what lies at the root of this relationship. They like to mix it up a bit in the sexual sense, and with both being so keen on all that's new and exciting, they allow their limitless imaginations free rein in order to invent original ways of bringing each other pleasure. Funny how they both feel safe in something strange and new, but that's because of their tight (and not just emotional) bond. Aquarians love to defy expectation, even to shock on occasion, and since nobody loves a surprise or catches on as quickly as a Gemini, it's sheer pleasure all the way for both of them. There are no dark corners or perplexing motivations in this relationship; just pure electricity to light up their libidos.

AQUARIUS MAN WITH **CANCER WOMAN**

 In love: From her viewpoint it appears to the Cancer woman that she looks after her Aquarius man in ways he doesn't even know he needs. She's so into mothering that she can be like a surrogate parent at times. But from his point of view, this can amount to smothering. It's not that he doesn't appreciate her efforts, but having been born under an Air sign, he needs to breathe and he likes his independence. He also likes to shake things up a bit, create some mayhem, and cause some shockwaves. Her watery nature is clannish and clinging, which means that she'll be the conductor to his electricity until the result is a raging, angry storm that has them both running for cover. He doesn't show his emotions openly and his aloof and dogmatic approach to life can irritate her. She may think he's simply cold and unfeeling. It's true that he's a cool Water-Bearer but even so, there's a part of him that might just need the Cancer lady's warmth. And there's a big part of her that revels in his colorful mind. He's never short of ideas and that feeds her creative spark. This is a union that could work out as long as they lay all their cards on the table so both can see what they're in for.

In bed: The Aquarius man needs to proceed with caution if he wants to open the Cancer woman's mind to some of the more diverse—she might say kinky—possibilities available to them as sexual partners. She needs to be cuddled and caressed and she doesn't normally like to be completely naked, but if he's patient and able to gain her trust, he could pull it off—along with her clothes. There is a strange fascination between these two and their sexual relationship could be deeply moving for them both. If she's willing to accept that he's not going to give an overt display of emotional commitment, and if he can work at being affectionate while also being sexually stimulating, then they could be surprised at how compulsive their lovemaking could be. Their lovemaking could very well become an extremely titillating pastime. If he would simply relax into the experience of being pampered, then her gentleness and soft caresses could drive him wild with excitement rather than simply excite his irritation. They won't find it easy to understand one another without words but if they can spell out their needs and wants, this will not only be the precursor to some wonderful lovemaking, but will also bring them closer to a divine sexual experience.

AQUARIUS MAN WITH **LEO WOMAN**

In love: As opposites in the zodiac, the Leo woman and Aquarius man will be drawn to one another immediately, like a magnet to metal. When they meet, it's spellbinding, enchanting, and instantly intriguing. Her fire and glamour act like a beacon to him; he feels truly privileged to have gained her attention and it makes him tingle all over to have it focused on him exclusively. She, meanwhile, is fascinated by his every move and hangs on his every word. He's an intelligent man, always clever with words, and she'll be a rapt and ardent listener. At the beginning, he'll play the prince, sweetly taking her hand in his and gently strolling off with her toward a blissful, romantic union. But later on, if her displays of jealousy become too frequent, they'll bring most Aquarius men out in a rash, while his overemphasis on the intellectual will have a cooling effect on the Leo lady's passion. Both need frequent time to themselves and really appreciate the fact that, in this respect, they are so similar. But if they have too much time to themselves, they may eventually find their own niche somewhere else. When they're together, they'll always love and adore each other, but if they are allowed to drift and, heaven forbid, fall into the arms of another, there'll be no coming back. They both need to keep their loving bond strong. That way, it will always be alive and kicking.

 In bed: It's hard to describe the erotic energy between these two lovers because it's ethereal, unrepeatable, and sacred, but when they get into bed together, it's as if they're on another plane. With Aquarius, the Leo woman becomes an earthy seductress who exists simply to be pleasured, and he kisses her with such ardor and *amour* that her Lion heart races as it never has before. But there are also extremes within this relationship; he has the ability to bring her to the farthest possible reaches of heavenly ecstasy and she can make this often cool and aloof man as hot as hell. Sometimes things can be decidedly cool, but when that happens no one should take offense. For example, the Aquarius man sees talking as the precursor for excellent sex and does a lot of talking, while the Leo woman may view this as lacking in spontaneity—too much discussion and not enough action. However, he never fails to give her good sex when she least expects it! Theirs is really an unpredictable match, but when they get their magnetic vibrations humming on the same frequency, they could have the most electrifying sex of their lives. On the other hand, when they're not in tune, it could take all the power in the national grid to turn them on. However, he can be detached and she needs the odd lazy moment to relax and recharge her batteries, but they'll be prepared to put up with the so-so, because the good is so, so good.

AQUARiUS MAN WiTH ViRGO WOMAN

In love: The Virgo woman and Aquarius man will be totally intrigued by each other and could build up a fairly powerful connection based solely on a mutual need for stimulating conversation. The two of them will spend many a night curled up on the sofa, high on the excitement of tearing apart and putting back together conceptual ideas about the meaning of life and the universe. It makes her feel really special to have this knowledgeable man so intently focused on what she's saying; it means the world to her to be appreciated for her mind rather than her body. But though there's much that she admires in this man, and he in her, neither of them are well enough equipped to get into each other on every possible level. Both are truly independent, he perhaps more than she might expect, and this could lead to great expectations and little fulfillment. They both tend toward detachment, aloofness, and respect, so, although making a lasting emotional connection might take quite some time, if they both hang in there, they'll suddenly find that they've developed a rather steady devotion to one another. But it's not easy for them to recognize whether they really feel something special for each other until it's perhaps too late. This is not one of those partnerships that just feels right from day one, but it's never really wrong either. It needs time and tenacity; eventually, the truth will out.

In bed: It's a mutual mind thing between the Virgo woman and the Aquarius man. They're so attracted by each other's seemingly detached sexuality that it raises their expectations and libidos to high-voltage levels. When these two get into bed together, toys come in very useful. Not only do they help to satisfy their sexual needs, but they also provide hours of fun afterward when they take them apart to see how they work! This is sex, but not of the conventional sort. They both enjoy what it has to offer, and bed is the place where the Virgo woman will feel the deep connection to the Aquarius man that isn't all that evident during their conversations. He'll be totally turned on by her ability to light his fuse and she'll surprise him with her zealous hunger for his body. These two could reach stratospheric levels of erotic exploration when they're in bed together but it would require some lateral thinking on both their parts and a willingness to cater to each other's needs. She must have him totally, physically with her, and wanting and needing her; only then can she reveal to him just how deep her sexuality goes. She expects a lot from him but he'll quickly learn to live up to all her expectations!

AQUARiUS MAN WiTH **LiBRA WOMAN**

 In love: Since both of these people were born under Air signs, this is one very stimulating relationship. These two could sit and shoot the breeze together until the cows come home. The Aquarius man may not be the most romantic guy in the world, but he's zany and funny and the Libra lady finds him very attractive. He's also extremely receptive to her romantic ideals, because she doesn't load them with a heap of sticky emotions that would make him feel uncomfortable. At first, he connects with her on the level of friendship and although she may have to lead him up Lover's Lane, he'll certainly be fascinated enough to follow. She'll never be in any doubt that he finds her infatuating, and once she has grabbed his attention, she'll find that it's completely focused on every little thing she does. The Libra lady loves to talk and conceptualize and the Aquarius man loves it just as much, so these two can get into some really good conversations, exploring all the fabulous ideas that occur to them. He may sometimes take the high moral ground and try to tell her how to think, but she's clever enough to get her own point across. They'll both be totally delighted with the knowledge that, in loving one another, they've also found a friend for life. There exists a level of comfort and compatibility between these two lovers that simply can't be experienced by ordinary earthlings. This lucky couple will really hit it off and probably never have to come down from their clouds again.

 In bed: The Aquarius man is inventive—the Libra lady might even say a little kinky—but that shouldn't give her pause because here's a guy who'll listen to the fantasies that she whispers in his ear and will make them come true. She'll tell him that it's only with him that she wants to act out her fantasies, and that will really get him going! He needs her to flirt with him before he'll make a move, but since she loves to flirt that won't be a problem. Though she won't have the same quantity of romps with Mr. Aquarius as with some other men, she'll certainly have quality! Sometimes he'll do things to her that she didn't even think were possible, let alone sexy, while at other times he'll get her in the mood on the phone while he's on his way home, and then get distracted and not come back for hours. But she probably won't mind because, in the meantime, she'll either have been on the phone to someone else and will have forgotten all about his little telephone tease, or she'll have accepted an invitation to meet up with a friend instead. If she's really missing him then she should check out his toy cupboard. If he happens to walk in and catch her, then the games really will begin, for this guy can give a truly electrifying performance.

AQUARIUS MAN WITH SCORPIO WOMAN

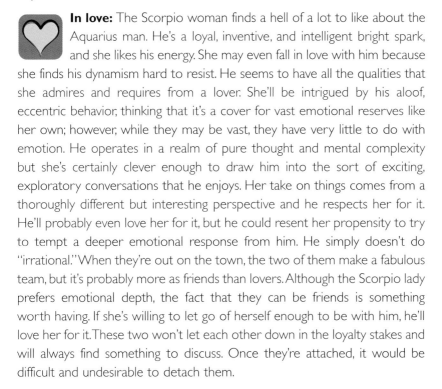

In love: The Scorpio woman finds a hell of a lot to like about the Aquarius man. He's a loyal, inventive, and intelligent bright spark, and she likes his energy. She may even fall in love with him because she finds his dynamism hard to resist. He seems to have all the qualities that she admires and requires from a lover. She'll be intrigued by his aloof, eccentric behavior, thinking that it's a cover for vast emotional reserves like her own; however, while they may be vast, they have very little to do with emotion. He operates in a realm of pure thought and mental complexity but she's certainly clever enough to draw him into the sort of exciting, exploratory conversations that he enjoys. Her take on things comes from a thoroughly different but interesting perspective and he respects her for it. He'll probably even love her for it, but he could resent her propensity to try to tempt a deeper emotional response from him. He simply doesn't do "irrational." When they're out on the town, the two of them make a fabulous team, but it's probably more as friends than lovers. Although the Scorpio lady prefers emotional depth, the fact that they can be friends is something worth having. If she's willing to let go of herself enough to be with him, he'll love her for it. These two won't let each other down in the loyalty stakes and will always find something to discuss. Once they're attached, it would be difficult and undesirable to detach them.

In bed: Strange sex! There's no other way to describe the Scorpio woman and Aquarius man's sensual coupling. If strange sex appeals to them both, and chances are that it will, then their bedroom experience could go on for longer than anyone expects, least of all themselves! The Aquarius man is different from any other lover that the Scorpio lady has ever had. He can be so inventive that he makes the *Kama Sutra* look like a boring "how-to" manual. But he might not have it in him to get this woman's juices really flowing because his package doesn't come with the emotional investment she needs. She doesn't simply want technical know-how and clever tricks that are designed to bring her to orgasm; she must have intense, deep, searing passion. But she'll certainly want to get it on with him because he has an intriguing allure and she's into losing herself in a variety of ways. But once may be enough. He'll be excited by her eroticism but may drown in her sea of emotional sensuality, for the Aquarius man can only do emotions in a mechanical kind of way and will back off when he finds it too difficult to keep up. As an Air sign, not being able to breathe or think his way through an experience means that he's unable to access his mental fantasies, and that's where he finds the most potent sexual satisfaction.

AQUARiUS mAN WiTH **SAGiTTARiUS WOmAN**

 In love: There's a natural affinity between the Sagittarius woman and the Aquarius man. She'll give him all the freedom and independence that he wants and will support his solo endeavors.

For his part, he won't restrict her desire to explore and experience life to her heart's content. Each has a deep respect for the other's need for fulfillment as an individual, so a loving bond will grow between them as they realize what a rare and special person they have found and how much rarer and more special they have become as a result of their alliance. This is a relationship where they can be fully themselves. There's no need to put on airs and graces to impress each other; he loves her just the way she is and vice versa. He won't buy her flowers or whisper sweet nothings in her ear, but neither will he be insincere or untruthful about what she means to him. The Aquarius man's love is honest and friendly. They can't fail to inspire wondrous new thoughts and ideas in each other and will really connect and grow into one another, so much so that, on evenings when they were just going to sit and have a little chat, by the time they think about going to bed, the sun will be high in the sky. Their excitement at indulging so wholeheartedly in fascinating, mind-expanding conversations is such that the air will crackle around them. They'll never get bored with each other unless she's the type of Sagittarius who's addicted to the gym or he's the type of Aquarius man who's married to his computer.

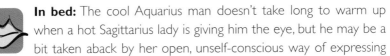 **In bed:** The cool Aquarius man doesn't take long to warm up when a hot Sagittarius lady is giving him the eye, but he may be a bit taken aback by her open, unself-conscious way of expressing her sexual desire. He can't quite believe that his fantasy woman is actually there next to him, in the flesh! But will he be able to tame this wild, wanton

creature? Does he really want to? She certainly gets his eroticism going and she'll find that he makes love as much with his mind as with his body. Her fiery, adventurous nature inspires him to try ever more different ways of bringing her pleasure. She'll test his inventiveness to the limit, which is exactly what he needs to stay interested, so together they'll discover some truly unusual ways to make love. He can be a touch selfish but the idea is that if she watches him, she'll be encouraged to do the same—a mutual turn-on! When he puts in a particularly good performance, the type that has her screaming "encore," he might get a little cocky, but she'll take control of the situation and they'll soon be rocking the night away, then singing like canaries once again with the rising sun.

AQUARIUS MAN WITH **CAPRICORN WOMAN**

 In love: On a mental level, the Aquarius man is a truly stimulating partner for the Capricorn woman and on a spiritual level they can really connect. But on the physical and emotional levels, she could very well scare the hell out of Mr. Aquarius. Her type of intensity makes him feel obliged to live up to her high expectations and even if it's all only in his mind, he can find it very restricting, particularly when he's in a gregarious, lighthearted mood. He doesn't bow to authority and prefers to break the rules rather than make them, while she'll never know whether she's coming or going and she can't look to him for answers because he has no idea what she's talking about. However, if the aloof Mr. Aquarius and the cool Ms.

Capricorn do develop a fondness for each other, it will be a profound and strong one. Without him even realizing it, she'll help tame his wayward drift—though she'll never change him. He'd never agree to that! He does have a genuinely loyal streak and will devote his heart, at least, to her, while she'll give him some tolerance, which is the final ingredient that's needed for a very perfect, palpable romantic mix. They'll never get bored when they're talking about the important, earth-shattering subjects they find of interest, and when they're joking and playing around together, they really make a connection, since both find life and themselves a little absurd. From there on, love can crystallize into something quite beautiful and long-lived.

 In bed: What an intriguing lover this guy is. One minute he can't get enough of his lovely Capricorn lady, the next he's on automatic pilot, his mind is way out there, and she might as well be with a dummy! But the Aquarius man can be an inventive, original lover so she'll never be bored even though she won't always recognize the man who's lying next to her in bed. This could be exciting or confusing, depending on her mood. He'll soon realize how important foreplay is to the Capricorn woman, and how much time he needs to invest in stoking up her erotic passions, but this is something he can do very well, particularly when he's getting the right response. But just when he's built her up to a crackling electrical storm of pleasure, he could get distracted, flip the switch, and short-circuit, and then it will be Ms. Capricorn's turn to blow a fuse. Their differences could make the lovemaking unpredictable, and the Capricorn woman prefers to know what's going to happen next, but the Aquarius man will quite naturally raise her temperature so, for better or for worse, she'll definitely get hot. What they do have in common will be enough to keep them together. It's hardly ever the same each time they bump into one another, so instead of things grinding to a halt, variety will be the spice of their sexual life.

AQUARiUS man WiTH **AQUARiUS WOMAN**

See pages 71–73.

AQUARiUS man WiTH **PiSCES WOMAN**

In love: When the Aquarius man meets Lady Pisces, he's full of wonder and curiosity because he's easily seduced by anything he can't figure out. He takes pride in his intellect but when the mysterious Pisces woman walks into his rational realm, he's completely bamboozled. She is eager to please and is drawn to his charismatic friendliness and sharp perception. Although mentally and spiritually they share some accord, when it comes to the emotional world, they are galaxies apart. But these two connect on the level of cosmic consciousness rather than on that of the mundane world. Given time, they can work together beautifully for the Aquarius man learns fast—even when it comes to learning not to try to figure her out—while she melds perfectly into his world—the way a lake hugs the rocks on a shore. However, she has to have faith that he is a rock, because he won't ever say so. That would be too much like committing himself to one single form of expression. Meanwhile, she needs to let the waters of her emotional ocean gently wash over him instead of trying to immerse him because, if she does, he'll just roll away. He's certainly loyal, but he needs all the space in the universe in order to express himself, his loyalty, and his love in his own way. These two will adore each other forever, but without trust that adoration will only exist on some other plane.

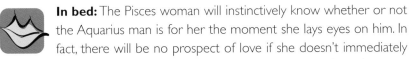 **In bed:** The Pisces woman will instinctively know whether or not the Aquarius man is for her the moment she lays eyes on him. In fact, there will be no prospect of love if she doesn't immediately feel some chemistry. Eternal intrigue is what keeps the Aquarius man interested, so he may hold back a bit to see if the electricity between them has the power to turn them both on and light up their libidos. However, if she's in any doubt, there's one surefire way to find out, and that's to strip off and jump in at the deep end. She'll either be left breathless and frantic for more lovemaking or desperate to pull out the bait. He's emotionally aloof while she rates a ten on the scale of romantic sensuality, so this could cause problems for the Lady Fish who wants to take her Water-Bearer lover deep down to swim in a limitless sea of erotic and emotional feeling. He can do erotic and limitless well enough, but for him it has to be on a stratospheric, fantasy level, high above the clouds, where he won't drown in pleasure but will be inspired by the stars he sees before his eyes. Sexually, this is an all-or-nothing coupling—all they have to do is try it once.